MOTHER
HUBBARD
LOVE

IN MEMORY OF
MY MUM AND DAD

Oxford University Press
First published 1986

ISBN 0 19 558150 4

Printed in Hong Kong
Published by Oxford University Press
5 Ramsgate St, Auckland 5, New Zealand

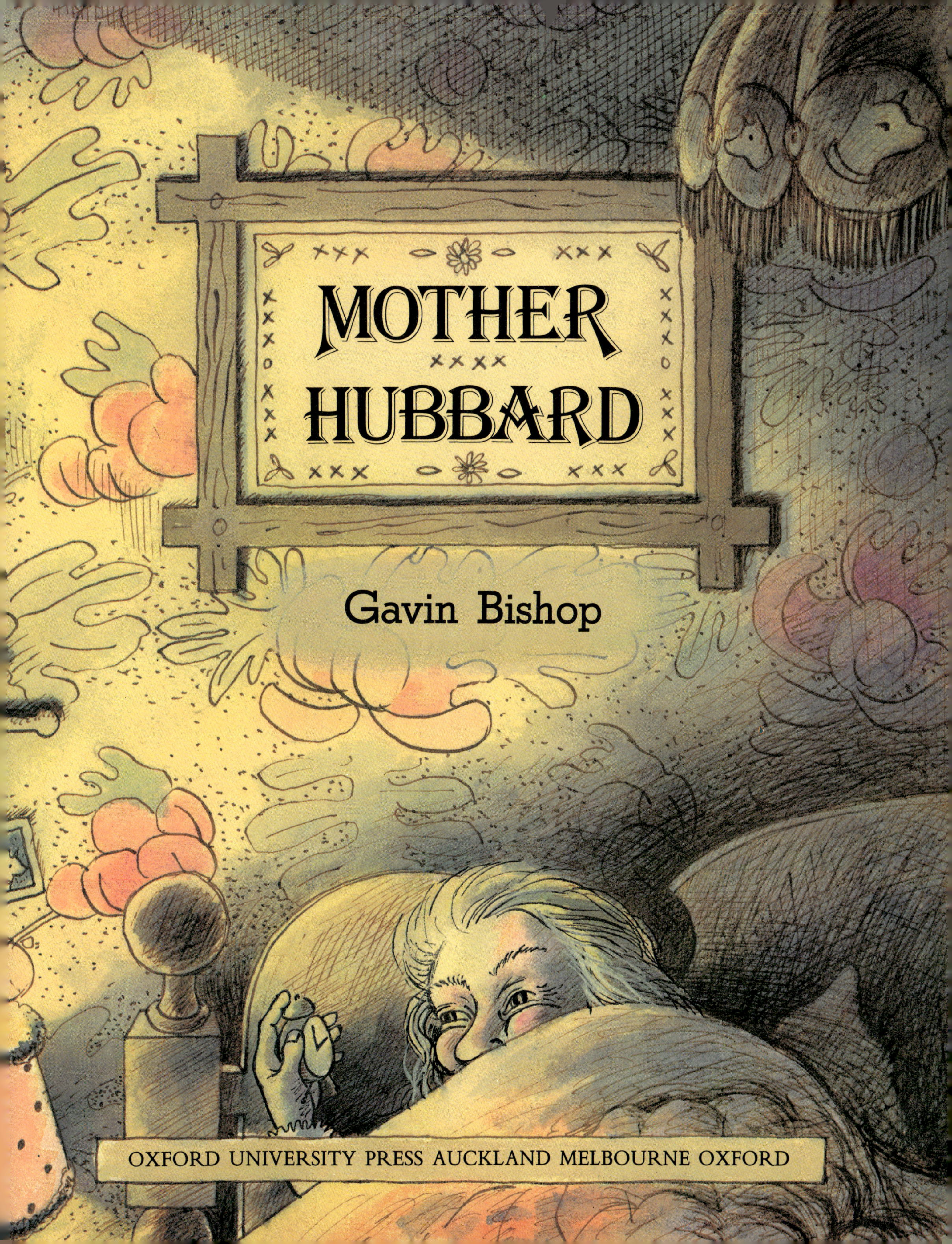

MOTHER HUBBARD

Gavin Bishop

OXFORD UNIVERSITY PRESS AUCKLAND MELBOURNE OXFORD

Old Mother Hubbard
Went to the cupboard,
To get her poor dog a bone:
But when she got there,
The cupboard was bare
And so the poor dog had none.

She went to the baker
To buy him some bread;
But when she came back
The poor dog was dead.

She went to the undertaker
To buy him a coffin;
But when she came back
The dog was laughing.

She took a clean dish
To get him some tripe;
But when she came back
He was smoking a pipe.

She went to the alehouse
To get him some beer;
But when she came back
He sat in a chair.

She went to the tavern
For white wine and red;
But when she came back
He stood on his head.

She went to the fruiterer
  To buy him some fruit;
But when she came back
  He was playing the flute.

She went to the tailor
To buy him a coat;
But when she came back
He was riding a goat.

She went to the hatter
To buy him a hat;
But when she came back
He was feeding the cat.

WIG

She went to the barber
To buy him a wig;
But when she came back
He was dancing a jig.

NEWS
MUSICAL DOG TO WED?

She went to the cobbler
  To buy him some shoes;
But when she came back
  He was reading the news.

She went to the draper
To buy him some linen;
But when she came back
The old dog was spinning.

She went to the florist
  To buy him a rose;
But when she came back
  He was dressed in his clothes.

The dame made a curtsey,
The dog made a bow;
The dame said, 'Your servant,'
The dog said, 'Bow-wow.'

This wonderful dog
  Was Dame Hubbard's delight,
He could read, he could dance,
  He could sing, he could write;
She gave him rich dainties
  Whenever he fed,
And erected this monument
  When he was dead.